INTRODUCING MEDIA STUDIES

Newspapers

NANCY BUTLER

Series Editor: David Butts

HODDER AND STOUGHTON
LONDON   SYDNEY   AUCKLAND   TORONTO

ACKNOWLEDGMENTS

The author and publisher would like to thank *The Fife Leader* for kind permission to reproduce illustrations on pages 11, and 13; the *Glenrothes Gazette* for photographs on pages 6, 24, 26, 28, 31 and 35; *The Daily Mail* for the article on p. 31; Popperfoto/Reuter for the photographs on pages 38 and 39; *The Scotsman* for the photograph bottom right of p. 40; Barnaby's Picture Library for the remaining three photographs on p. 40; Associated Press Ltd for the photograph on page 41.

British Library Cataloguing in Publication Data

Butler, Nancy
    Newspapers.
    1. Newspaper publishing industries
    I. Title   II. Series
    338.4'7070572

    ISBN 0 340 41135 X

First published 1989
Third impression 1990

Typeset by Rowland Phototypesetting Ltd, Bury St Edmunds, Suffolk
Printed in Great Britain for Hodder and Stoughton Educational, a division of Hodder and Stoughton Ltd, Mill Road, Dunton Green, Sevenoaks, Kent by
St Edmundsbury Press Ltd, Bury St Edmunds, Suffolk

Contents

NOTE TO THE TEACHER

This book not only describes the newspaper industry, it also includes information about the many factors influencing the production of a newspaper and its success in attracting readers. Individual pupils and groups are encouraged to find out information for themselves, and to put a number of practical and analytical skills into practice. Discussion will be an integral part of the course.

Equipment itself need not be elaborate. Each pupil or group will require some sort of workbook or project folio. And the usual supply of paper, pens, pencils, glue, rulers etc. shouldn't be too difficult to provide. A tape recorder, camera, typewriter and telephone would be useful, if available. You will also need a dice for each group in the Paperchase Game.

It is essential that you have a very large collection of newspapers to hand. Enlist the help of your pupils. It shouldn't be long before you have a wide and varied collection to choose from.

The pupils are encouraged to conclude the project by compiling a class newspaper. But this is by no means the most important task. The investigation and the analysis are just as important, and you might feel that they alone are enough to provide an insight into the industry – especially if time is limited.

This is only one approach. In the end, as always, it is up to you, the individual teacher, to use the material as is most appropriate with your particular class. All the best.

Key to logos

 a practical activity in pairs or groups

 thinking activity

 activity where photocopying is permitted

 activity to be written into notebooks

 activity for group discussion

The Newspaper Business

MONEY, MONEY, MONEY

If a paperboy or girl delivered 125 newspapers every day for 1,000 years, he or she would deliver over 45 million newspapers in all. That's a lot of newspapers and a lot of work. But the astonishing fact is that those 45 million newspapers can be sold throughout Great Britain in one day . . .

Think about it. How much money would you make if you sold those 45 million newspapers at twenty pence each?

Yes, you're right! You would be a millionaire in one day! It sounds very attractive, doesn't it? Look at these circulation figures:

Name of newspaper	Number of newspapers sold each day*
Daily Mirror	3,121,454
Daily Record	767,000
The Times	442,375
Sun	3,993,031
Daily Star	1,288,583
Daily Express	1,697,229
The Standard	522,407
Daily Mail	1,759,455
Daily Telegraph	1,146,917
The Guardian	493,582
The Independent	292,703
Sunday Mirror	3,018,910
Sunday People	2,932,472
Sunday Mail	876,000
News of the World	4,941,966
Sunday Times	1,220,021
Sunday Express	2,214,612
Sunday Telegraph	720,902
The Observer	773,514

* *Average figures for the period July to December, 1987.*

Wouldn't you like to own a newspaper? Perhaps you think that you would be very good at it, choosing the news and sports reports and articles that would appeal to everyone. Do you think that you would be able to tell everyone working on your newspaper what to do and what to say? Before you decide, read on. This book aims to give you some interesting information about the demands and challenges you might face in the newspaper business.

WHY READ NEWSPAPERS?

Why do we have newspapers at all? In some ways they can seem very old-fashioned: after all, it is easy to listen to news bulletins on our radios, or watch events almost as they happen on the television. Why wait until the following day to read about an event that most people have already heard about?

First of all, newspapers are much more convenient than radio or television.

You can read a newspaper where or when it suits you – in bed, in the train, on the beach. You don't have to miss any of the story if you are interrupted, because you can go back to read it later. And if you don't understand what you've read, you can read it again.

Secondly, newspapers have the space to include far more detail than time will allow on radio or television. Often radio and television news can only give people the bare facts: *what* happened. For example, the TV newscaster might announce that a revolution has broken out in Afghanistan and show the viewers dramatic pictures. Next day, however, your newspaper will give far more detail, discussing the reasons *why* the Afghans are fighting, and explaining *how* the revolution is affecting other countries.

Thirdly, newspapers which are printed near your home might include local news which is interesting to your neighbours. The rescue of Mrs Smith's cat, or the fight to prevent a new by-pass going through your front garden, is highly unlikely to be included in the television news. But it is important news to you.

Of course, we don't have to wait for our newspaper to be pushed through the letterbox. We can buy a paper at any time from the local newsagent or from a street vendor.

TYPES OF NEWSPAPER

Can you recognise different types of newspaper? There are five main types and they are:

Dailies	newspapers sold throughout the country every day.
Weeklies	newspapers addressing readers in one particular area of the country which are usually printed once a week.
Evening papers	are sold in the afternoon, giving all the latest local news and some national news.

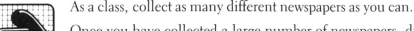

Sunday papers	are printed for leisure reading at weekends with longer articles and often a colour magazine.
Free local advertisers	newspapers delivered weekly to people in one area, containing local news and lots of local advertisements. These are delivered to your house free.

 As a class, collect as many different newspapers as you can.

 Once you have collected a large number of newspapers, divide into groups. Your teacher will give each group some of the newspapers. As a group, try to decide which newspapers are *dailies*, *weeklies*, *evening papers*, *Sunday papers* or *free local advertisers*. Once you are satisfied, report your findings to the class. Your teacher could record the results of each group on the blackboard.

 IN YOUR WORKBOOK, make a note of this information. Hand the newspapers back to your teacher; they can be used later on in other activities.

Discussion

The newspaper's printed name on the front page is called a *banner*. What do the newspaper banners in your collection tell you about the type of paper it is?

ATTRACTING THE READER

In 1702 there was only one daily newspaper. Now there are lots and people can choose which newspaper they want to read. If you are the owner of a newspaper (the *proprietor*) and people don't read your paper, then you don't make any money. Your newspaper will soon have to close down. So, newspapers are competing with each other, trying to attract you, the all-important reader. Each newspaper must appear to offer more than other similar papers on the news stand, or at the newsagent. Most importantly, the front page must be eye-catching because this is the first thing you see. The headlines on the front page are designed to attract your attention.

Headlines

HEADLINES ATTRACT ATTENTION

especially if they fill most of the front page or if they are likely to shock or anger readers.

You have probably noticed that different newspapers put the same news stories into a different order of importance. The headline on the front page not only attracts your attention, it also tells you which story is most important to that paper. It must make this story appear the most interesting story of the day to you, the reader, as well.

Divide into groups. Your teacher will give each group a small number of daily newspapers. (Each group should have the same papers, printed on the same date, for the sake of discussion – but this is not absolutely necessary.) Newspapers tend to be printed in two sizes:

Broadsheet	a large size newspaper, often with smaller print
Tabloid	a smaller size newspaper, easier to hold

(i) As a group, divide your papers into two piles – larger and smaller.

IN YOUR WORKBOOK. Record the group's findings as follows:

Tabloid	*Broadsheet*
The Sun	The Times

(ii) Now, as a group, look carefully at the headlines on the front page of each of the newspapers. Some newspapers use really large headlines; some use smaller headlines.

Once again, divide your papers into two piles. This time, put the papers with really large headlines on one side, and those with the smaller headlines on the other side.

IN YOUR WORKBOOK. Each person should now record the group's findings as follows:

Large Headlines	Smaller Headlines
The Sun	The Times

In your group consider the two sizes of newspaper – which do you prefer? Why? Does everyone in the group agree?

Now compare the two tables in your workbooks. Are there any similarities? Why do you think this is?

Report your group's findings to the class. Are you in agreement with the other groups?

IN YOUR WORKBOOK, write a short paragraph stating which type of newspaper you would prefer to buy, and why.

Colour

Although most newspapers are printed in black and white, some do use one or two other colours to attract your attention – red especially. The first British daily newspaper to use full colour photographs regularly was started in 1986 by its proprietor, Eddie Shah. His idea was that the colour pictures would make people buy his newspaper because it would be much brighter and more eye-catching, more modern, more adventurous. However, his idea took a long time to be copied by the rest of the daily newspaper industry, because the new technology required to print full colour is very expensive. The name of the newspaper Eddie Shah started is *Today*. Would the fact that it is more colourful make *you* read it? Do you prefer a black and white newspaper?

Advertisements attract readers

You may be attracted to buy a newspaper because you want to read advertisements that interest you. Not only do advertisements attract readers, they bring in money for the newspaper; businesses and private advertisers pay for the space they take in a paper. The better known the paper, and the more readers it has, the more it will charge its advertisers for the space they use.

What services and goods do you often see advertised in the national daily papers? Would you look in your national daily if you wanted to buy something like a bicycle from someone in your area?

Readers attract advertisers

Imagine that you are selling 300 big teddy bears for Christmas presents. You want to charge £10 each. Obviously, you need to advertise, but you only want to spend about £50. There are five places you have considered advertising:

Shop window	500 people visit the shop weekly, with probably 350 of these people over 25 years old. Cost: £5 for one week.
Local weekly	read in 300 homes over a small area. Cost: £10 for one advertisement.
'Free' local weekly	delivered to 10,000 homes over a larger area, but estimated to be read by 24,000 people. Cost: £15 for one advertisement.
National daily	read in 1 million homes. Cost: £50 for one advertisement.
National magazine	read in 5,000 homes. Cost: £30 for one advertisement.

Discussion

In groups, discuss how best to spend your advertising budget of £50. And remember – think of good reasons for your decision. Discuss your decision with other groups. They might think your idea is silly. Prove them wrong!

Why is it free?

Some newspapers are put through your letterbox at home completely free. Opposite is the front cover of a free local weekly. This paper is delivered, it claims, to 48,000 homes each week.

Choose any daily newspaper from your collection and compare its front cover with that of the *Fife Leader*.

IN YOUR WORKBOOK, write down your answers to the following questions.

(a) What differences can you see between the two front covers?

(b) Why do you think the newspaper proprietor can afford to print and give away the *Fife Leader* for nothing?

Design an interesting advertisement

Design an advertisement of your own, suitable for either a national or a local newspaper. Keep in mind the following:

(a) What are you selling?

(b) What sort of person is likely to want to buy?

e.g. age, sex, social class?

(c) How much will it cost?

(d) Make it sound attractive.

(e) You can miss out information that might stop people from buying, but *don't* tell lies!

Variety

A newspaper doesn't just print news and advertisements. Readers want other things from a newspaper:

(a) **Information**: financial index, TV and radio guide, racing guide, sports news, arts reviews, fashion news, weather reports.
(b) **Entertainment**: cartoons, horoscopes, puzzles, picture strips, crosswords.

Can you suggest any other information that a newspaper prints?

If you look at newspapers regularly, which parts of them do you:

(a) look at first,
(b) always look at,
(c) always miss out?

Why? Do you enjoy reading what your friends enjoy reading? Or have you different preferences?

A *bit of a challenge!*

You may know someone who can't resist doing newspaper crosswords every day. Or you may have tried to do them yourself. Millions of people enjoy the challenge of testing their skill at the crossword every morning, and many newspapers give prizes for correct answers. And of course this means that people will buy tomorrow's issue as well, to find out what the answers were, and to try the new crossword. It's a bit of a challenge every morning, and crossword addicts don't want to miss it! Newspapers know this and employ people specially to make up crosswords and puzzles. Would you like to do this? Try the simple crossword opposite. Write your answers onto the photocopy of page 15 that your teacher will give you. The answers are on p. 48.

IN YOUR WORKBOOK. Design a simple crossword of your own. First choose five or six words that cross one another, sharing letters like the ones on the crossword that you have just filled in. Then make up clues to each of the words, giving the clue its line reference, for instance 2 across, or 3 down, and so on.

Try your crossword out on your friends and family. Try to complete one of the crosswords in your favourite daily paper.

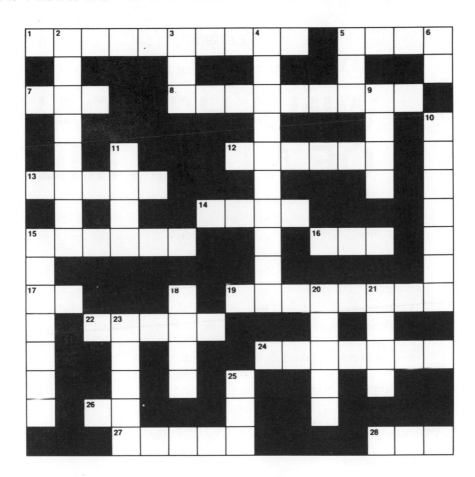

ACROSS

1 You need a camera to take this (10)
5 . . . . phone (4)
7 To hand over money for goods (3)
8 *The Guardian* is one (9)
12 Red is one (6)
13 These separate newspaper reports (5)
14 Short for information (4)
15 Another name for a paper sold once a week (6)
16 Initials of the National Graphical Association (3)
17 A reporter never takes this for an answer (2)
19 Business groups gather together at these (8)
22 Using ink to put letters on paper (5)
24 The smaller type of newspaper (7)
26 Short for advertisement (2)
27 Every reporter wants to be first with this (5)
28 Initials of the National Union of Journalists (3)

DOWN

2 Title at the top of a story (8)
3 A robber using this would be sure to be mentioned in the papers (3)
4 Popular name for the G.P.O. (4,6)
5 Where the headline goes (3)
6 Short for editor (2)
9 Make money (4)
10 Another name for papers sold each day (7)
11 To find a story, a journalist must do this (4)
15 People who come first in competitions (7)
18 A . . . . shot is a type of picture (4)
20 Meetings often take place round this (5)
21 Midday (4)
23 A person with a newspaper usually does this (5)
25 Opposite of night (3)

A *bigger prize!*

Win a fantastic new BMX Bicycle!

WIN A HOLIDAY OF A LIFETIME!

How would you like to win an adventure trip to some new and exciting place in the world? It sounds great, doesn't it? And so it should. It's yet another way to encourage readers to buy your newspaper.

Did you enjoy doing the crosswords in the previous activity? Would you have tried even harder to solve them if a large prize had been offered for the correct answer? Of course!

Who pays for the prizes? Often it is you, the reader. Buying more newspapers in order to enter the competitions means that you are increasing the amount of money that the newspaper makes. The extra money can be used as a cash prize or to pay for prizes that are to be given away, like the bicycle mentioned above. The newspaper has probably been given the bicycle free by a bicycle manufacturer. In return, its brand of bicycle gets a lot of free publicity.

WHICH NEWSPAPERS DO YOU READ?

Which newspapers are read by your family at home?

IN YOUR WORKBOOK
(a) Copy out the table below;
(b) fill in the boxes with the names of the types of newspapers read by you and your family.

DAILIES	WEEKLIES	EVENING EDITIONS	SUNDAY PAPERS	'FREE' LOCAL WEEKLIES

Class survey

Compare the newspapers you read at home with the ones read by your classmates and their families. Do they get the same papers? To show which newspapers are the most popular among the class, it would help to draw a bar chart.

Dailies

As a class, make a list of the different daily newspapers read each day by everyone, using the table in your workbooks. Ask your teacher to put the list on the board; it should look something like this:

The Sun   9
The Guardian   8
The Daily Mail   4
The Times   6

IN YOUR WORKBOOK, use your class list to draw a bar chart. (You might find it easier to use squared paper for this activity.) Mark the number of people in your class up the left, vertical arm of the chart. Write in the names of the newspapers your class reads along the bottom line. Use the chart below as a guide. It has been filled in using the results from the list of papers and readers above, as an example.

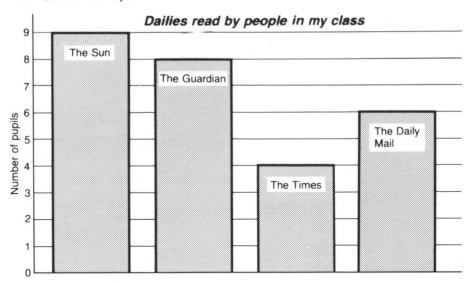

Compare your own chart with this example. Are they different or similar?

Sunday papers and local papers

1 Now do the same for Sunday papers that are read each weekend by members of your class and by their families.
2 And do the same for the different kinds of local papers (this can include weeklies, evening papers and 'free' weeklies).

WHICH NEWSPAPERS DO OTHER PEOPLE READ?

Survey

You might like to carry out a survey to find out what people outside your classroom read. Ask as many people as you can which newspapers they read each week. Ask friends of your family, relatives, teachers, neighbours.

IN YOUR WORKBOOK, record your results using a table like the one given below. You will probably find it easiest to lay this out on the long side of the page.

	Dailies			Sunday Papers			Local Papers		
	1st choice	2nd	3rd	1st choice	2nd	3rd	1st choice	2nd	3rd
Name									
Name									

When all your class are ready with their results, ask your teacher to help in preparing a list of how many people read which daily papers, which Sunday papers and which local papers.

IN YOUR WORKBOOK, present these lists as three bar charts, one for daily papers read, one for Sunday papers read and one for local papers read, as in the example on page 17.

Now answer the following questions.

(a) Which newspapers were the most popular in your class?

(b) Which newspapers were the most popular when you asked other people, outside your classroom?

(c) Compare your answers to (a) and (b). Do you notice anything?

(d) Which newspapers were the least popular in your surveys?

(e) Why do you think some newspapers are more popular than others?

(f) Would you say that different people buy different types of newspapers? Why?

'Quality' or 'Popular'?

Discussion

Newspapers are sometimes described as *popular* or *quality* papers. Using information you have found out from your personal reading, your class discussions and your surveys, decide:

(a) which papers you would describe as quality newspapers;
(b) which papers you would describe as popular newspapers.

IN YOUR WORKBOOK, write a paragraph saying which papers you have chosen for (a) and (b), and say why.

Getting the News

REPORTER

How do newspapers get their news? It might be news of the local charity event held at your school, reported for your local weekly. Or it might be news of events in the Far East, reported by the national daily paper you are reading. To make sure that it gets up-to-date news as it happens, a newspaper employs *reporters* whose job it is to find news stories and report them as interestingly as possible. You might like to become a reporter, either at home or abroad. There are three different jobs you can have:

(a) as a reporter employed full time in one area or country, by one newspaper;
(b) as a 'Stringer'; 'stringers' are people who used to be full time reporters, but now they just send reports on special subjects when the paper needs them.
(c) as a freelance reporter; freelance reporters do not work for any particular newspaper. They write reports on subjects that they feel are interesting and try to sell their work to different newspapers and magazines.

If you want to be a reporter, you will find it useful to be able to write in shorthand (a form of 'code' writing), which allows you to take notes very quickly. Reporters also tape speeches made by politicians, or interviews given to them by celebrities. Then they write up a story, making it as readable and eye-catching as possible.

The notes in normal writing might look something like this:

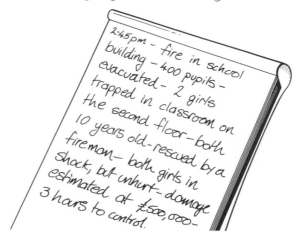

2.45pm - fire in school building - 400 pupils - evacuated - 2 girls trapped in classroom on the second floor - both 10 years old - rescued by a fireman - both girls in shock, but unhurt - damage estimated at £500,000 - 3 hours to control.

The Press Release

Sometimes, you wouldn't have to take notes. Instead you might be handed a 'ready-made' *Press Release*.

Discussion

Why do you think you might not be able to take your own notes? Can you suggest events and occasions when prepared notes would be given out to reporters?

Here is an example of a press release:

PRESS RELEASE

XIV Intercontinental Games
London 1988

ATHLETICS FLASH INTERVIEWS MONDAY 25 JULY, 1988

Stephen Connors

Stephen Connors has a throat virus, but his chances of recovering from Thurday's 400 m hurdles' final are good, said United Kingdom's manager, Graeme Leitch.

After Connors had appeared to finish his semi-final today in some distress, Leitch said: 'It looks like a little throat virus. He has been a little bit under the weather since about Saturday.'

He was asked about Connors' chances of running in the final. Leitch replied: 'He has a few days to recover, and his chances of recovering for Thursday must be quite good.'

Leitch praised Connors for winning the semi-final. He said: 'I think it is marvellous that Connors can do so well when he is not fully fit.'

N.W
25/7/88
Wembley

IN YOUR WORKBOOK, write a short report for your local weekly newspaper, or for your favourite national daily. Use either the written notes for the story about the fire, or the press release about Stephen Connor's illness.

But before you begin, stop to think! You have to catch your readers' attention. And you have to make them keep on reading your report to the end. Not only that, you have to give them facts as well. How are you going to do all this?

Keep these points in mind:
☐ Pick the fact you find most exciting and interesting and start with that.
☐ Make your sentences short, and use words which catch people's attention.
☐ Include what was said by people that you interviewed, if possible.
☐ Finish with a sentence which is interesting, unusual or surprising.

Look carefully at the two 'reports' opposite. Both describe the same school fire. What differences do you see between the two reports? Which report appears to be more eye-catching? Why?

At 2.45 pm today there was a fire in the local primary school main building where 400 pupils were at work as normal with their teachers. All the pupils had to be evacuated by firemen who came to put out the blaze, but 2 girls were trapped in a classroom, both 10 years old, and one fireman rescued them separately. They were shocked but not hurt. It took 3 hours to put the fire out and it caused a great deal of expensive damage which means that the school may not be able to open for some time.

Two 10-year-old girls were trapped on the blazing second floor of Moan Primary School this afternoon. 400 pupils were rushed to safety, while firemen wearing breathing equipment climbed to outside windows to snatch the terrified girls from the choking smoke. As they were carried down, onlookers dashed to help but were waved back by the Chief Fireman. The girls were taken away by ambulance, but a hospital spokesman later confirmed that, although they were very shocked, only their clothing had been burnt. The fire took 3 hours to put out and left firemen exhausted. The Head Teacher said: 'This has caused at least £500,000 worth of damage, and I really don't know how the school can re-open again until at least some of the repairs have been done. It looks as if pupils will be off school for at least a week, I'm afraid.'

Preparing your own report

Prepare a report of your own based on an event in your own school, town, or neighbourhood, e.g. school sports day, local fund-raising event, a new leisure centre recently opened. Use the guidelines below to help you.

Taking notes
IN YOUR WORKBOOK write down notes on:
(a) where it happened?
(b) when it happened?
(c) who was involved?
(d) how it finished? (e.g. money raised, winners' names)

Interviewing
Always try to interview at least one person who was involved. This might be the winner, the person who organised the event or who set up a new venture. To prepare for your interview:
(a) decide who to interview;
(b) make up your questions beforehand and write them down in your workbook;
(c) if you are taping the interview, prepare the tape recorder before you start recording. Wind the tape to the right place and make sure that the tape recorder is working properly! If you are taping outside, use an external microphone if you want to cut out a lot of background noise;
(d) arrange with the person to be interviewed when the best time for the interview would be.

Writing the report

Listen to your tape.
IN YOUR WORKBOOK, write down what you want to include in the report and add this to your notes on where and what happened. Now, write your report. Make it as exciting and interesting as you can.

COPYWRITER

Reporters must try to get their reports back to head office as quickly as possible.

How would you send your report if you were fifty miles away from your office? The quickest way is to send your actual typed report by FAX. A FAX machine sends your page, or pages, of typing directly over the telephone lines. It 'reads' the page, rings up your office FAX machine and sends the typing down the line as coded electronic impulses. At the newspaper office, you would see your page of typing appearing almost instantly, just as you can hear a voice immediately on the telephone. You can also send photographs like this. However, it may not always be easy to find a FAX machine when you are reporting 'in the field'. The easiest way then is to use a normal telephone and dictate your report to someone in the office. This person is called a *copywriter*. Copywriters type your report as you read it out slowly over the phone. Obviously, both reporter and copywriter have to be very careful that there are no mistakes in the report that the copywriter types. See how successfully you can dictate the report you have written.

Divide into pairs. Person A reads a report to person B. Person B writes down what person A says. People who are reading must remember to tell their partners *exactly* what to write, including when to use such things as full stops and capital letters. When this is done, compare the original report with the new copy.

Did Person A give clear instructions? Did Person B carry out the instructions correctly? How quickly was the report reproduced?

Now swap over!

If this can be done over a telephone, so much the better.

PHOTOGRAPHER

Have you decided whether or not you would make a good reporter? Or a good copywriter? Remember, that to do these jobs you would have to learn shorthand and typing – at speed.

You can, of course, become a *photographer* instead. The photographs produced by a newspaper photographer are expected to be of good quality even when they have been taken under difficult conditions. These pictures must also be better than those taken by other newspaper photographers . . .

Which photo?

In your groups, cut out all sorts of news photos from your newspaper collection. As a group, decide which photographs you think are better. Why?

Remember, of course, that these are the pictures which the newspapers *did* use. Lots of other photographs would have been rejected. If you have different newspapers covering *the same event*, cut out these pictures. Which do you think are better in this case? Why? Why do you think each newspaper chose the picture (or pictures) that they did?

IN YOUR WORKBOOK. Choose a photograph that you personally like. Stick it into your workbook. Write a paragraph saying what you like about this photograph, and why.

Illustrate your reports

If your teacher will allow, take some black and white photographs to go with one of the reports that you have written. If you were really employed as a newspaper photographer, your pictures would be developed very quickly. You will have to wait longer for your own – unless, of course, your school has a darkroom.

Discussion

Lay your photographs out on a table. In small groups discuss the following:

(a) did you include everything that you meant to show in your photograph?

(b) did you stand steadily enough to stop your pictures from blurring, even when you were in a hurry, or excited?

(c) did you use a flash, or set the camera correctly, for darker shots?

(d) which photographs are the best ones? Why?

(e) what difficulties did you have in taking your photographs?

(f) how could you improve on them next time?

Remember, as a newspaper photographer your pictures are expected to be better than everyone else's nearly all the time. If they are constantly boring and out of focus, then you won't keep your job for very long!

EDITOR

The *editor* controls a team of people, including, for instance, the news editor, foreign editor, picture editor, city editor, gossip column editor, women's page editor, literary and arts editor and financial editor. Each member of the editor's team chooses which stories should be covered in his or her section of the paper. But there might not be room for all the stories. The team therefore meets the editor to discuss the way the newspaper is progressing, to sort out any problems and to be kept up to date with the editor's opinions on news stories. These meetings are held at least twice a day.

The editor will then decide:

(a) where everything goes in the newspaper;

(b) which stories to use;

(c) which stories should go on the front page, and

(d) how the front page should be presented.
    This is known as the *layout*.

Editors also comment on items in the day's news about which they feel very strongly. These written comments are published in the paper, and are known collectively as the *editorial*. Almost all daily newspapers have an editorial. But these might not be on the same page in all newspapers, and it is not always obvious that an article is in fact an editorial. Look out for words in the headline like 'comment', 'what the *Daily Moon* says . . .' or the editor's name. The editorial is one part of the paper which is based more on opinion than on fact. For this reason the article may deliberately support one rather than another side of an argument. By looking closely at the editorial, the reader can identify the kind of opinions the newspaper as a whole is likely to support.

SUB-EDITORS

As the day progresses, the city editor, sports editor and everyone else on the editorial team are collecting stories for the next day's paper. At last, the editor and his team agree on the importance and placing of each report and story. They now make up a plan for every page in the newspaper. These plans have very little detail; in fact, in some cases, they might look like a page of squiggles.

It is the job of the *sub-editor*, or 'sub', to choose the headlines for each report, to cut and correct the stories and features to fit the page and to supervise the final preparations of the newspaper layout. A sub-editor can drastically change what a reporter has written, sometimes for the better, sometimes for the worse. Subs work through the night, under the night editor and the chief sub-editor, until the last edition of their paper has been printed.

Column inches

You can tell how important the editor feels a report is by the amount of space it has been given in a newspaper – especially if it is on the front page.

Newspaper pages are divided into columns. The space taken up by a report is expressed in '*column inches*'. You can see this laid out for you in the picture below. The column inches include photographs and the headline.

Look at any page in a newspaper. Can you find the columns? How many are there? Are there the same number of columns on every page?

Discussion

Can you think of a reason why newspapers might have columns? Why do you think that some newspapers use more columns on pages where there are advertisements? Who, do you think, wants these extra columns?

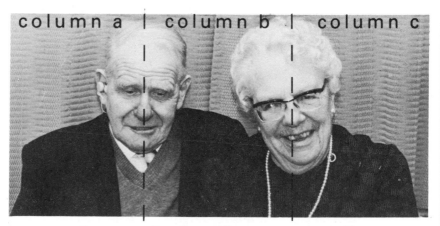

column a | column b | column c

Joy night for couple

WHEN Markinch couple, George and Christina Nicholson, celebrated their Diamond Wedding on Saturday night, it was like the real thing all over again.

For on hand to wish them well at the party in the Galloway Inn were their best man and bridesmaid.

Mr and Mrs Nicholson of 43 Commercial Street, Markinch, were married on November 25, 1927, in the Portland Bar, Commercial Street, a few doors away from where they now live.

Christina (85), whose maiden name was Kinnear, was born and has always lived in the same house at 43 Commercial Street.

Before her marriage she worked in Balbirnie Wool Mill.

George (88), was born in Milton of Balgonie and was a miner for 30 years.

He served with the Seaforth Highlanders in the First World War and was wounded at the battle of Arras in France in 1917.

Our picture shows the happy couple with their telegram from the Queen.

The story with the greatest number of column inches is the most important story on the front page. And since it is on the front page, it is possibly the most important story in the whole newspaper. Some papers continue their main story on other pages if there is not enough room on the front page. This also allows the front page to have more and/or larger headlines and pictures. It is often these which attract readers to buy one particular paper.

IN YOUR WORKBOOK, copy the table below. Now look at any newspaper of your choice from the class collection. Use *only* the front page and measure the number of column inches in each story, to fill in your table.

Name of newspaper ....

Date ....

Reports on front page:

| Title | Column inches taken: | | Is the report continued on another page? |
	headlines & pictures	written report	
....	....	....	....
....	....	....	....
....	....	....	....

(*and so on for as many reports as there are on the front page*)

Now underline the title of the story with the most column inches on the front page. Write a paragraph saying why you think the editor chose to make this story the most important.

How would you like to be editor?

Here are three lists of news items. Imagine that you are the editor of a large national daily.

IN YOUR WORKBOOK, place the stories in the order of importance you would give them, with the most important story at the top of the list.

1 A   Bank robbers shoot at police
   B   School pupils get longer holidays
   C   World champion boxer knocked out
   D   General Election. Who will form the new government?

2 A   Tourists see Loch Ness monster
   B   TV starts a Channel 5
   C   Queen to visit Australia
   D   Motorway crash, two killed, seven injured

3 A French millionaire's son kidnapped
   B Russians land on Mars
   C Heavy snow in NE England, hundreds stranded
   D Famous filmstar marries

Discussion

Discuss your results with your classmates. Why did you put your stories in this order? Did your friends choose the same or a different order? Why? Is it possible that you can *all* be right?

Type

Decisions must now be made about the way the printing on the page is going to look.

Lettering in newspapers is called the *type*. But there are different styles of type used throughout a newspaper. The most obvious example of the role of different *typestyles* is in the headline. We have already discussed the fact that headlines are intended to attract your attention. The type used is often very large, plain and bold, easy to read from some way away. But not only can you change the size of the type, you can also change the shape and design of the type. There is more scope for altering typestyles in the expensive newspapers, like a Sunday paper for instance, but the type is chosen to fit the 'image' that the newspaper wants you to have of the subject.

Here is a product called
Kaxon Running Shoes

Here is a company called
Kaxon Fine Art Publishers

Both the product and the company have the same name, Kaxon. However, the typestyle used for each version of the name Kaxon alters the reader's image of the same name.

IN YOUR WORKBOOK, try to write the word Kaxon in six different ways, to represent six different products or companies of your own choice. Ask a friend to say what sort of product or company your typestyle represents. Did they get the right answer straight away?

Now look at one of your big national daily papers. Compare the typestyles used on the arts review page with those used on the sports or financial pages.

TYPOGRAPHERS AND COMPOSITORS

Until recently, the type would usually be chosen by a person known as a *typographer*. He or she would also work out the length of lines, length of report and the actual size of the headline. It would then be up to the *compositor* to position large blocks of metal type and picture blocks to make up a page to be used for printing.

Over the last few years, compositors have begun to use computers to choose typestyles. The typographer is no longer required to choose the metal type; the compositor can select typestyles by computer codes, and can also assemble, edit and change the appearance of the page without moving from the computer keyboard. This makes the job quicker, an important thing to keep in mind in the newspaper business.

Pictures in newspapers

Look at any newspaper photograph really closely. It is made up of many little dots. Can you see them? You might find that you have to use a magnifying glass to see them.

The dots are there because the original photograph has been changed into a printed picture made up of a series of tiny dots. A real photograph cannot be used directly on the paste-up because all that would appear when the paste-up was reproduced would be a very blurred image. Each photograph has to be turned into something that can be printed onto normal, non-photographic paper. To do this, a *halftone screen* is used. Can you find out how the halftone process works? (A diagram and an example are given overleaf.)

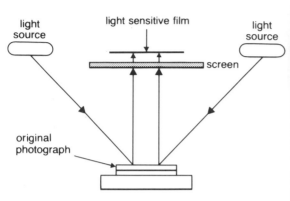

PASTING UP THE PAGE

The type has been chosen, the text has been typeset, the photographs are printed as halftones and the artists have finished their drawings and cartoons. All the elements of the newspaper have been prepared and are now ready to be pasted up.

The person who does this job makes a 'master' for each page of the newspaper by sticking all the material for each page onto a single sheet of paper. Each page will follow the editor's plans showing where every report, photograph and drawing should be. The *Paste-up artist* must make sure that everything is stuck down in the correct place, that no large blank spaces are left, and that nothing is crooked.

This is quite a painstaking task, requiring patience and an eye for detail. And the paste-up artist has to work fast; the newspaper must be printed and in the shops by the next morning . . .

Your paste-up

You could try pasting up some of the reports written earlier by you and your classmates.

In groups.
(a) Place the reports in order of importance.
(b) Get a large sheet of paper.
(c) Divide the sheet of paper into columns.
(d) Decide where the reports will go – write them out in columns. Better still – get them typed if you can.
(e) Decide on the shape and size of both headings and headlines.
(f) Position the photos and/or drawings.
(g) Have you included everything?
(h) Could anything be improved? (e.g. check for gaps, articles overlapping, headlines much too small.)
(i) Glue everything onto the large sheet of paper.
(j) Are you satisfied?
Have you drawn lines between the different reports?
Have you written a few words underneath each of the pictures (the captions)? No? Do it now.

PRINTER

Once the newspaper has been pasted up it is ready to be printed. The printer's job is an interesting one – one which you might enjoy.

First, the printer photographs each pasted-up page of the newspaper. But the photograph is not then printed on paper as you might expect – it is printed on a thin sheet of plastic. At this stage it looks very strange because it is a negative. This means that where the letters and black parts of the news photographs were, the negative print shows white. The white blank spaces on the page and the photographs show black on the negative.

This is an example:

Second, the printer places the negative on top of another sheet. This sheet is made of metal covered with thick plastic. A special light is shone through the negative sheet as it lies on top of the metal and plastic sheet. Where there are white words or areas on the negative, the light goes straight through it and eats away the plastic covering the sheet underneath, exposing the metal in the shape of the words. The light doesn't go through the black areas on the negative. You could try some printing of your own, using a potato. See below.

Make a 'potato' print

CUT A POTATO IN HALF

USING THE POINT OF THE KNIFE, CUT THE SHAPE OF A LETTER ON THE POTATO

CAREFULLY SCOOP AWAY THE PART SHADED BLACK.. A DEPTH OF 3-5 CMS SHOULD BE ENOUGH

PAINT THE AREA AROUND THE LETTER TRYING NOT TO GET PAINT IN THE PART THAT YOU HAVE CUT

PRESS ONTO A SHEET OF PAPER

REPEAT TO MAKE A PATTERN. BE CAREFUL NOT TO PUT THE POTATO ON TOP OF A LETTER THAT YOU HAVE JUST PRINTED

DELIVERING THE NEWS

Once the page plate is made, the newspaper is ready to be printed on special machines called *presses*. Some presses, nowadays, can print 60,000 newspapers, 48 pages long, in one hour. A newspaper plant with ten presses can print over 4 million newspapers between ten o'clock at night and five o'clock the next morning.

To speed things up, machines automatically put the pages in the correct order, as well as fold, cut, count, bundle, tie and label copies of the newspaper, ready to be sent out to newsagents throughout the land.

Of course, these 4 million newspapers have to be delivered quickly too. Those which have to travel the greatest distances are obviously despatched first. These newspapers will most probably do some of their journey by train, or even possibly by plane.

Newspapers which travel shorter distances usually go by road. Most newspaper groups have their own fleet of vans and lorries to do this job.

Some changes might be made to the newspaper throughout the night. There is a chance, therefore, that your newspaper will look slightly different from the one received by a friend 500 miles away.

By six o'clock in the morning, most newspapers will be in the shops ready to be sold to the customer.

What is News?

The first element of a newspaper report is, as we have already seen, its headline, which is designed to attract your attention. Headlines are short, the type used is big, and their use of words is as economical as possible.

People do not actually need every piece of a phrase or sentence in order to make sense of what they read. In headlines, words which can be assumed are missed out.

Headlines can therefore convey information in a kind of shorthand which we now read automatically. Headline writing today is an essential element of a report, intended not only to convey information quickly and dramatically, but also to present a point of view forcefully. Look at the headlines below:

U.S.S.R. RESCUE BID
(*Newspaper 1*)

Soviet government moves troops to Middle East
(*Newspaper 2*)

RUSSIANS INVADE!
(*Newspaper 3*)

These headlines all report the same incident. However, the way each has been composed immediately tells you how the reporter or newspaper is going to present the significance of the incident.

IN YOUR WORKBOOK, answer the following questions:

Which newspaper appears to:

(a) agree with what Russia is doing? Which word tells you this?
(b) disagree with Russia? Which word tells you this?
(c) report what is happening, but without taking sides (*Neutral*)? Can you point to any one word which tells you that the report is neutral? If not, why do you think this is?

WHAT IS THE REPORT TELLING YOU?

Read the two reports which follow carefully.

Star opens Brigtown leisure centre

Brigtown's new, architecturally renowned leisure centre was opened yesterday, much to the delight of a crowd of over 4,000 spectators. Soap opera star and heart-throb, Wayne Nelson, was there to perform the opening ceremony. He entered the sun-kissed building to hearty salutes from the crowd, using a gold key, hand-crafted especially for the occasion.

As Nelson signed autographs after the ceremony, he commented, 'Gee, I just love the place – especially the swimming pool. It's like a championship pool, but without the starkness. I was really tempted to jump in.'

Councillor Smith, who has now fought for the construction of the leisure centre for 3 years, told reporters, 'It is a credit to the city. Progress has at times been slow, but now that it is open, people will soon realise just how much the local people will benefit from such marvellous facilities.'

Designed by Adam Clark, the building has already been commended for two international awards. Centrally situated, facilities include a purpose-built gymnasium, an Olympic-size pool, a sauna and an indoor running track. It will be open to members of the public daily, from 8am to 9pm.

Residents lose leisure centre battle

Residents of Park Square, Brigtown were saddened yesterday at the opening of the city's £5,000,000 leisure centre. For 18 months Bob and Margaret McLellan have held public meetings, been to court and held demonstrations in their Square, in an attempt to alert the council and the public to the serious housing problem in Brigtown. Margaret told the press yesterday, 'My daughter, Susan, put her name down on the council list for a house two years ago. But there are few houses to be got. There are over 500 names on the waiting list.' Bob added, 'What do the council do? They use land to build a leisure centre. You can't live in a leisure centre.'

Susan McLellan was married in January of this year, but the couple are still without a home of their own. At the moment they share a room in the McLellans' house. But not all residents are as lucky as Susan.

Councillor Bett, when asked to comment, said, 'Our housing budget is limited, but already in this year, we have built 50 houses in Fairness Road. The leisure centre is a bonus, partly built with subsidies from the government. The rest of the money came from the leisure budget.'

The Brigtown Housing Association plan to send a petition with over 5,000 signatures to the Prime Minister at the end of the week.

Both reports are concerned with the opening of a leisure centre in Brigtown. However, the articles are written in two entirely different ways. If you saw only one of the reports, you would have difficulty in immediately recognising any bias – especially in the first article. It is only when you see the two together that different facts and opinions emerge in connection with the opening of the leisure centre.

Discussion
In groups, discuss the following points.

1a The first article describes the opening of the centre. How is the centre made to sound appealing to the reader? Pick out words to back up what you say.

b How much attention is given to the views of the people opposed to the opening of the centre? Why? Do you think this is wrong?

2a The second article concentrates on Brigtown's housing problem. What is its connection with the new leisure centre?

b How is the reader made to feel sorry for people like the McLellans? Pick out words and phrases to back up what you are saying.

c The other side of the argument appears to have been covered in the article. How? How do we recognise the fact that this side of the argument is not supported by the newspaper?

3 Compare the headlines. Which headline obviously supports the opening of the leisure centre? Pick out the word (or words) from the headline which tells you this. Which words attract attention in the other headline? What do they suggest to you? Why?

IN YOUR WORKBOOK. Following the discussion, write notes on each of the above questions in your workbook.

No doubt you will have noticed that bias can be achieved in a number of ways. Articles can be biased by:

A missing out the opposite point of view entirely;

B appearing to support both sides of the argument, but emphasising one point of view instead of covering both sides equally;

C using words and phrases which deliberately praise or condemn.

BIAS IN WRITING

You might like to try your own hand at writing a report which supports a particular viewpoint. Here are some notes on an incident in Laird's Carpet Factory. Read it through, and then choose a partner as you will be working in pairs.

Place:	Laird's Carpet Factory
Time:	Friday, 12th March – 12.30pm to 4.30pm
Incident:	10 factory workers stopped working – police called – 2 factory windows broken – scuffles – 1 policeman injured, 1 worker injured
Reasons given:	
factory workers:	factory very cold (53°F, 12°C) all morning – not the first time that this has happened – people off work with colds and 'flu beforehand, workers can't work efficiently.

factory owner: person in charge of heating given orders to use less oil for heating, to save money – company short of money – difficult to pay wages and buy fuel too, saving on fuel is preserving jobs.

One person in each pair should now write a report, using the notes above, which supports the workers' view of the incident.

The other person writes a report, using the same notes, which supports the factory management's view of the incident.

Both members of each pair should decide on their own headline as well.

Now, compare your reports. What tone does each report adopt? Are both reports using emotional vocabulary to convince the reader of their individual viewpoints?

Compare articles

As a class, collect as many different daily and evening newspapers, all printed on the same day, as you can.

Look for the same story on the front page of each newspaper; it is likely to be the major news event of the day. Cut out each paper's version of the story and stick all the articles onto a large sheet of paper. Make sure the right paper's name is written next to its article.

IN YOUR WORKBOOK, copy out the table below and use it to compare the articles. The first column is filled in for you as an example.

Name of newspaper	Incident being reported	Length in column inches	What the headline says	Words from the report which might make the reader angry or shocked or upset	Does the report appear to support someone or something (yes or no)?	If you answered yes, who or what does the report seem to support?
Daily Telegraph	Strike	24"	Air traffic controllers say 'enough'	Collision, confusion, near-miss, dangerous	Yes	controllers

Answer the following questions:

(a) what differences can you spot between the articles?
(b) what similarities can you see between the articles?

BIAS IN PHOTOGRAPHY

You have seen that the way a report is written can influence your view of the events it describes.

You may feel that photography, at least, can be relied on to show you the facts. Photographs show us exactly what has happened. Or do they?

Newspaper editors choose the photographs that they use very carefully. They select the picture, or pictures, that they want to use according to the impression they give of the subject. In order to be able to give their editor a good choice of pictures to select from, photographers take lots of pictures. The editor will use only two or three of them.

Look at the pictures and headlines below. Which picture would go best with each of the headlines? Which picture and headline do you think the most effective of the four?

Floods make thousands homeless
FAMINE TO FOLLOW FLOOD
Roof~top vigil for flood victims
FLOOD VICTIMS FLEE CITY

Anchorage

A picture on its own tells us little. Look at the picture below. You might think that these people have won lots of money. Someone else might think that lots of money has been raised for charity.

The newspaper must tell the reader exactly what is going on in its pictures. The words underneath pictures are called the *caption*.

For example the caption for the picture above could have been either:

LOCAL MAN WINS THE JACKPOT or **JOHN BLOGGS DONATES £1,000,000**

Adding a clear caption to a photograph is known as *anchorage*. Just as a boat cannot move away from the spot where it has dropped its anchor, the reader cannot stray very far from the meaning given in the caption.

Write two different captions for each of the pictures on the next page: your teacher will provide you with a photocopy of the page.

1 ....

2 ....

1 ....

2 ....

1 ....

2 ....

1 ....

2 ....

Discussion

When you have finished doing the captions for these pictures, compare your ideas with those of other people in your class. How different or similar were their captions? Did you see new meanings in these pictures when you read other people's captions?

Using a collection of different newspapers, find a photograph that interests you and cut it and its caption out. Write down the caption in your workbook. Now cut that off too. Ask others in the class to make up a new caption for your picture. Compare their suggestions to the actual caption used by the newspaper editor. Were these the same or quite different?

Cropping

Editors don't always use the whole of the photograph they have chosen. The picture you see in your paper is often *cropped*, that is, strips of the original picture have been cut off from the sides, top or bottom. This is done to focus attention on the part of the picture the editor feels is important. It is also done to try and fit a large picture into an already well-filled page!

So, although the camera doesn't tell lies, by cropping a part of the photograph you can change the meaning or emphasis of the picture.

Look at the two versions of the photograph below:

A

B

Discussion

Imagine that the newspaper you edit is writing a report on the homecoming of soldiers from a war.

1 If your reporter gave you an article stressing that the returning soldiers were conquering heroes, and telling the reader of the joy of reunion between soldiers and their families, which version of the photograph would you use: A or B?
2 If the article was critical of the war and talked about the sadness of maimed lives, which version would you use: A or B?

Discuss how, in this photograph, cropping can alter the audience's view of the emotion it shows. In the cropped photograph B, do you immediately notice that the soldier has only one leg? Would you say that the photograph without the crutch was telling lies?

Owning a Newspaper

In the newspaper world, at the moment, there are three very important owners (or proprietors) of newspaper groups. They are Robert Maxwell, Rupert Murdoch, and Robert Matthews. Between them, their corporations sell two-thirds of *all* the national daily and Sunday papers sold in Great Britain. This, you would think, would make them very powerful and very rich indeed. It certainly does.

Look carefully at the table below. You will see that Messrs Maxwell, Murdoch and Matthews all have money invested in a large number of businesses and corporations, other than in the newspaper industry. Because of this, these men cannot spend every day in the newspaper offices. Instead, they have to leave the organisation of the day to day business to other people.

Corporation	Proprietor	Newspapers	Other interests

Maxwell Communications Corporation	Maxwell	Daily Mirror
		Sunday Mirror
		Sunday People
		Daily Record
		Sunday Mail
		(Total circulation:
		  11,000,000)
			Central Independent TV
			Pergamon Press
			E. J. Arnold (furniture)
			Jet Ferry International
			  (Panama)
			Mares Australes (Chile)
			Hollis Plastics

News International	Murdoch	News of the World
		The Times
		Sunday Times
		Times Educ. Supplement
		The Sun
		(Total circulation:
		  10,200,000)
			Satellite TV
			Collins (Fontana)
			Channel Ten 10 (Sydney)
			Ansett Transport
			  (Australia)
			News Eagle (oil) (Australia)
			Whitefriars Investment

Fleet Holdings	Matthews	Daily Star
		Sunday Express
		Daily Express
		The Standard
		Morgan–Grampian
		  Magazines
		(Total circulation:
		  7,100,000)
			TV–AM
			Specialist Publications
			Capital Radio
			M G Insurance
			JBS Properties
			Lefpalm Ltd

If, like the proprietors mentioned in the table above, you had other interests and had to leave your new newspaper for long periods of time, how could you ensure that your policies were carried out? First of all, you would probably put your editor on a short term contract. If this editor failed to do what you wanted, then you could find a new editor after only a short time. Secondly, you could employ people who had the same beliefs and ideas as yourself. Thirdly, you could promote or reward people who really impressed you. And, wherever you happened to be working in the UK, or even abroad, you could always get hold of a copy of your newspaper and find out what was happening!

Staff structure on a newspaper

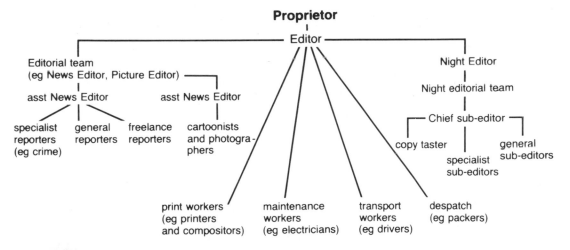

Discussion

In your group, look at a number of newspapers produced by one newspaper group, for instance Rupert Murdoch's News International.

Consider the following questions.

1 Can you see any similarities in approach between these newspapers?
2 Do you think that the proprietor's other interests will affect the newspaper corporation in any way?

Be prepared to discuss your group's findings and decisions with the rest of the class.

RULES OF THE INDUSTRY

By now you will have realised that the life of a newspaper proprietor is not an easy one. And in many cases the proprietor also has other businesses to look after, as you have seen. On top of all these responsibilities you, as proprietor of your paper, must make sure you follow special rules that all those working in the newspaper industry have agreed to recognise.

Four of the most important laws a newspaper proprietor must observe are:

(a) The Official Secrets Act
(b) The Prevention of Terrorism Act
(c) The Law of Libel
(d) The Law of Contempt

Below are listed the meanings of these 'rules'. In small groups, match each rule to its meaning:

(a) If a person is in court, newspapers can report what is happening. The report given cannot, however, say whether the reporter or anyone else working on the newspaper thinks that the person is guilty or not. This is because such reports might influence the opinions of people in the jury.

(b) Newspaper workers must not have any contact at all with people who are known to kill for political reasons, e.g. the IRA.

(c) People who work for the Queen or for the Government must not give out information about their work to the public or press unless it has been officially released for publication. If official information is leaked, it is an offence for newspapers to report it.

(d) Newspapers cannot print deliberate lies. This means that they cannot include nasty reports about the lives of people the newspaper does not like unless they have proof of what they are saying.

Can you find out what the penalties are for breaking these laws?

The Press Council

The Press Council is a voluntary body which was set up in 1953 as a 'press watchdog'. If you want to complain about something in a newspaper or the conduct of a journalist, the Press Council will help you free of charge, and may even offer you assistance with any expenses if you need this. The Council may try to negotiate a settlement between you and the editor of the newspaper you are complaining about. If a settlement cannot be agreed, the Press Council will judge the dispute and say whether it upholds your complaint. If the newspaper has also libelled you, however, you must agree not to take legal action if the newspaper agrees to publish the Press Council's decision.

If you want to use The Press Council's services, all you need to do is write to the director for a leaflet on how to make a complaint.

UNIONS

One of the functions of a union is to help employees who have problems at work; there are different unions for people who do different jobs in the newspaper industry.

Union members vote on any decisions arrived at by the owner or the union representatives. If the union cannot agree with the owner, then its members may come out on strike. This could stop the newspaper from being printed and sold.

To stop this happening, some newspaper groups have no unions. And obviously, the owner has a greater say in what employees must or must not do. Do you think that having no unions is a good idea?

Recently, new machines have been introduced into newspaper production plants. They allow news to be produced much more quickly. However, this has meant that some people have had to lose their jobs. For example, computers have removed the need for typographers and pasting-up, whilst machines can now count newspapers, a job which used to be done manually.

Of course, the unions try to protect their members' jobs. They know that it can be very difficult to find replacement jobs for people who have special skills, like pasting-up the front page of a newspaper.

But the newspaper owner also has a difficult decision to make. Does he or she buy new computers and machines to get news into newspapers quicker than everyone else? Or should all the employees be kept on, even if it means slower production and fewer newspapers sold?

Remember, if the owner does nothing to help employees who are affected by new technology, their union can stop the newspaper from making any money at all. But, if the newspaper group does not keep up to date, it will be unable to compete with all the other newspapers on the market. It might have to close down, and then everyone will be out of a job.

What would you do if you were the owner?

THE PAPERCHASE GAME

In groups, try your luck in the newspaper industry by playing *The Paperchase Game*. Your teacher will provide you with dice. Make your own counter from a small piece of card with your name on it. Good luck!

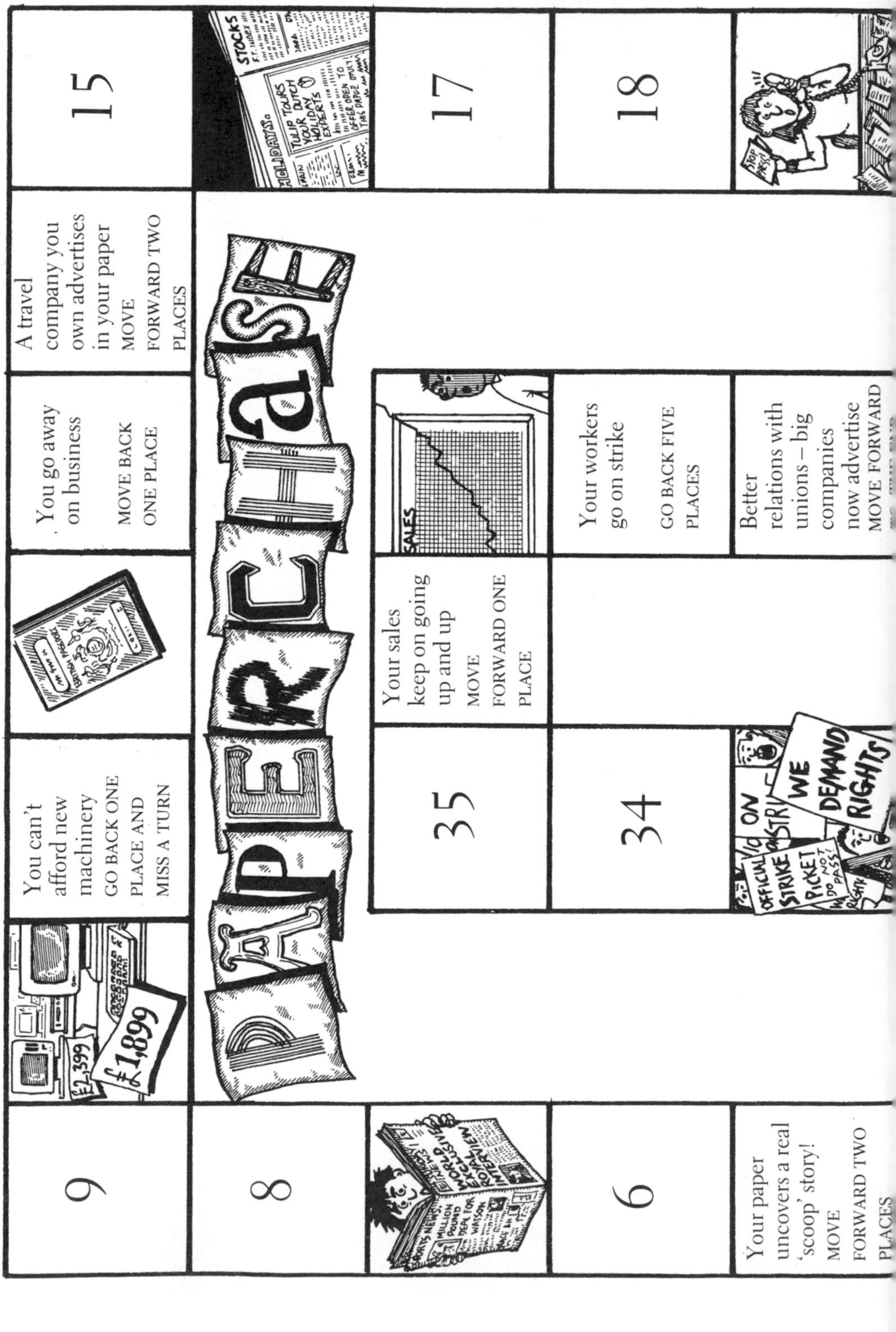

PAPERCHASE
9
£2,399
£1,899
You can't afford new machinery GO BACK ONE PLACE AND MISS A TURN
You go away on business MOVE BACK ONE PLACE
A travel company you own advertises in your paper MOVE FORWARD TWO PLACES
15
STOCKS
HOLIDAYS
TULIP TOURS YOUR DUTCH HOLIDAY EXPERTS
17
18
8
WORLD EXCLUSIVE ROYAL INTERVIEW
MILLION POUND DEAL FOR WATSON
SPORTS NEWS
6
Your paper uncovers a real 'scoop' story! MOVE FORWARD TWO PLACES
SALES
Your sales keep on going up and up MOVE FORWARD ONE PLACE
35
34
OFFICIAL STRIKE
PICKET DO NOT PASS!
WE DEMAND RIGHTS
Your workers go on strike GO BACK FIVE PLACES
Better relations with unions – big companies now advertise MOVE FORWARD

GO BACK ONE PLACE

SOLICITOR

22

You begin to sell Sunday papers – a slow start
GO BACK ONE PLACE AND MISS A TURN

GO BACK TO 5!

Your Sunday paper is popular

MOVE FORWARD TWO PLACES

You break the law of libel

MOVE BACK FIVE PLACES

SUNDAY NEWS SOLD OUT NO PAPERS

You sack your editor

GO BACK ONE PLACE AND MISS A TURN

EDITOR VACANCY

29

28

Your uncle leaves you a newspaper plant MOVE FORWARD ONE PLACE

No newspaper plants for sale

THROW A SIX TO MOVE

START

Throw a six to start

Your Own Class Newspaper

How about creating your own class newspaper? As a class, decide what size and what length your newspaper will be.

Start by appointing people to the jobs listed in Chapter 2, then move into production – but watch out for the pitfalls that we talked about in Chapter 3.

Give your newspaper a name and print enough copies for your intended readership: yourselves, other classes, teachers, friends and relations.

Did you make a profit? Your newspaper probably didn't make you enough money to buy a national paper for yourselves. However, with your experience, who knows what you might achieve some day.

Solution to crossword on p. 15

Across
1 Photograph
5 Tele
7 Pay
8 Newspaper
12 Colour
13 Lines
14 Info
15 Weekly
16 NGA
17 No
19 Meetings
22 Print
24 Tabloid
26 Ad
27 Story
28 NUJ

Down
2 Headline
3 Gun
4 Post office
5 Top
6 Ed
9 Earn
10 Dailies
11 Seek
15 Winners
18 Snap
20 Table
21 Noon
23 Reads
25 Day